NAVY

SEALS

BY NICK GORDON

BELLWETHER MEDIA · MINNEAPOLIS, MN

EPIC BOOKS are no ordinary books. They burst with intense action, high-speed heroics, and shadows of the unknown. Are you ready for an Epic adventure?

This edition first published in 2013 by Bellwether Media, Inc.

No part of this publication may be reproduced in whole or in part without written permission of the publisher. For information regarding permission, write to Bellwether Media, Inc., Attention: Permissions Department, 5357 Penn Avenue South, Minneapolis, MN 55419.

Library of Congress Cataloging-in-Publication Data

Gordon, Nick.
 Navy SEALs / by Nick Gordon.
    p. cm. – (Epic books: U.S. military)
 Includes bibliographical references and index.
 Summary: "Engaging images accompany information about Navy SEALs. The combination of high-interest subject matter and light text is intended for students in grades 2 through 7"–Provided by publisher.
 Audience: Grades 2-7.
 ISBN 978-1-60014-825-5 (hbk. : alk. paper)
 1. United States. Navy. SEALs–Juvenile literature. I. Title.
 VG87.G67 2013
 359.9'84–dc23

Printed in the United States of America, North Mankato, MN.

TABLE OF CONTENTS

SEALS

The Navy SEALs are an **elite** fighting force. They carry out **special operations** for the

SEAL FACT

SEAL stands for "Sea, Air, and Land." Navy SEALs operate in all of these environments.

Navy SEALs go through years of intense training. They learn to fight and survive in any conditions.

SEAL FACT

The hardest part of SEAL training is Hell Week. SEALs train with almost no rest for five days and five nights.

NAVY SEALS

Founded:	1961
Headquarters:	Coronado, California Little Creek, Virginia Pearl Harbor, Hawaii
Motto:	"The Only Easy Day Was Yesterday"
Size:	Around 2,500 active personnel
Major Engagements:	Vietnam War, Operation Urgent Fury, Gulf War, Afghanistan War, Iraq War, War on Terror

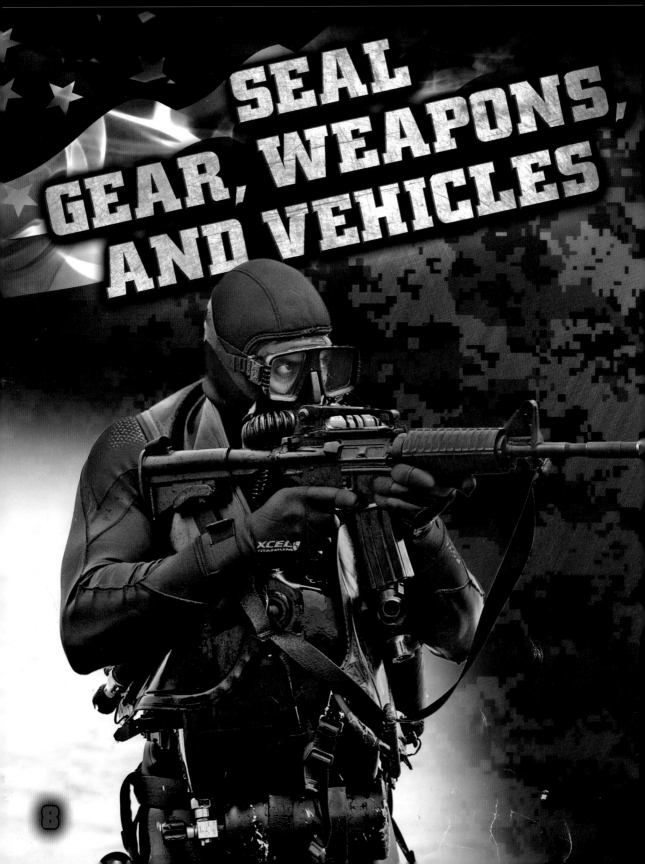

SEAL GEAR, WEAPONS, AND VEHICLES

SEALs need the right gear to perform their **missions**. They use parachutes to jump out of planes. **SCUBA gear** lets them breathe underwater.

SEALs use many weapons. Most carry a handgun and a rifle. Some carry **sniper rifles** and heavy machine guns.

SEALs carry knives to use in hand-to-hand combat.

SEAL FACT

SEALs often wear camouflage to blend in with their surroundings.

ROCKET LAUNCHER

Sometimes SEALs use explosives. They may carry **grenades** or **rocket launchers**. Powerful rockets can destroy enemy tanks.

Vehicles take SEALs to their missions. Small boats and helicopters move SEALs from Navy ships to shore. The SEAL Delivery Vehicle travels just below the surface of the water.

SEAL DELIVERY VEHICLE

15

SEAL MISSIONS

The Navy sends SEALs on its toughest missions. SEALs are often used to stop **terrorists**.

SEAL FACT

The Navy SEALs are split into nine teams. Each team has between 200 and 300 members.

SEALs gather information about enemies in **recon** missions. They may also carry out quick strikes against enemy bases or weapons.

SEAL FACT

The SEALs' war cry is *Hooyah!* They shout this during their training.

SEALs rely on teamwork to perform their missions. They work together and trust one another. They do whatever it takes to complete their missions.

GLOSSARY

elite—the most skilled

grenades—small explosives thrown by hand or launched by grenade launchers

missions—military tasks

recon—secret observation to gather information about the enemy

rocket launchers—weapons that fire explosive rockets

SCUBA gear—equipment that provides divers with oxygen to breathe underwater; SCUBA stands for "Self-Contained Underwater Breathing Apparatus."

sniper rifles—very accurate long-range guns

special operations—tasks beyond the duties of regular military personnel

terrorists—those who perform violent acts to create fear among people

TO LEARN MORE

At the Library

Besel, Jennifer M. *The Navy SEALs*. Mankato, Minn.: Capstone Press, 2011.

Gordon, Nick. *U.S. Navy*. Minneapolis, Minn.: Bellwether Media, 2013.

Yomtov, Nel. *Navy SEALs in Action*. New York, N.Y.: Bearport Pub., 2008.

On the Web

Learning more about Navy SEALs is as easy as 1, 2, 3.

1. Go to www.factsurfer.com.

2. Enter "Navy SEALs" into the search box.

3. Click the "Surf" button and you will see a list of related Web sites.

With factsurfer.com, finding more information is just a click away.

INDEX